The Song of the Climate Change—

Every Country Has Its Stanzas

The Long Darkness and the Light

*The eternal word,*
*the One God, the Free Spirit,*
*speaks through Gabriele,*
*as through all the prophets of God—*
*Abraham, Job, Moses, Elijah, Isaiah,*
*Jesus of Nazareth,*
*the Christ of God*

*The Song
of the Climate Change—
Every Country Has Its Stanzas*

*The Long Darkness
and the Light*

*God-Father, the eternal All-One,
gave a revelation in June 2019
through His prophetess and emissary
Gabriele*

Gabriele
Publishing House

## The Song of the Climate Change— Every Country Has Its Stanzas
## The Long Darkness and the Light

*Am, who I Am, the God of Abraham, Isaac and Jacob, the God of all true prophets and prophetesses, the God of all righteous men and women.*

*Throughout all the times of times, I, the All-One, sent beings from the Eternal Kingdom to My sons and daughters who had turned away from Me, the eternal Love, because they wanted to fashion the eternal law and thus, the Kingdom of the Being, in another way, according to their desires and notions.*

*I had given to the sons and daughters in the Fall-procedure a quantum of drawing and creating energies to take with them, so that they could show Me and prove to Me how it could be better.*

*The drawing and creating energies given to take with them for their own fashioning notions were, of course, a loan and not a gift, because the eternal law is absolute unity. Therefore, in the long run, there can be no divided creation. The eternal law is also absolute freedom, which is why they were given the possibility to prove that they can do it better than I, who I Am, in unity with the drawing and creating basic powers of the Eternal Kingdom, of Order, of Will, of Wisdom and of Earnestness, and of the filiation attributes of Kindness, Love and Meekness.*

*Despite the unimaginable Light-Ether of energy, which the renegades had received from the eternal, fine-material kingdom to take along with them, from the outset, the loan—the energetic creation-energies—was transformed down, all the way to the emergence of density, matter, and to further degenerations.*

*Since from the very beginning of their Fall, it became clear that it was exceedingly difficult for them to transform the energies of the Light-Ether back up, I repeatedly sent divine heralds, prophets and prophetesses, to the renegades.*

*How the fallen descendants of the eternal Kingdom dealt with these, their brothers and sisters from the eternal Being, is shown by their self-chosen patriarchy, the Moloch of the guild of priests and the state power.*

*The exorbitant abuse of energies—and this, from the very beginning—has not been nullified, for energy cannot be lost, neither the energies from yesterday nor those of today.*
*The negative energies are potentiated according to the so-called causality, also in terms of the same and similar patterns and behaviors, and this, of any kind.*
*The causal chain of the crimes of violence under the abuse of My name is also apportioned as energy to each one proportionately, also to the respective country and its inhabitants. Every link on the causal chain potentiates its unatoned energies or lessens them, which can also take place*

*through the incarnations in the respective periods of time.*

*All the crimes of violence against children, women and men, against animals on the Earth, in the Earth and above the Earth, as well as in the oceans, rivers and lakes have not been nullified. Everything that has not been expiated remains in the chain of causality.*

*No energy can be lost—even if the human being does not believe in My words.*

*The one who believes so-called worldly science, which likewise assumes that no energy is lost, ought to ask himself the question: Where are the energies that were created from person to person during the times of times, and this, throughout the generations? One question could follow the other: Who created what, and where have the energies gone?*

*Who was it yesterday, and who is it today?*

*It was the human being yesterday, and it is the same sinner today.*

*From the very beginning of the Fall, the Fall-experts wanted to prove to Me, the God of Abraham, Isaac and Jacob, the God of all the emissaries sent by God, that they could put My loan, the mighty drawing and creating Light-Ether, to use in their allegedly correct way, and increase it accordingly.*

*During the times of times and into the present time, My divine messengers, prophets and prophetesses, came to the "Fall-beings" and then, to the human beings. Other righteous men and women also brought them the bread of life, the law of the love for God and neighbor.*

*In all the times of times, the renegades—whether still Fall-beings or already human beings—chose their idolatrous gods, which they adorned with all kinds of gewgaws, embellishments and "dignities," raising them in a facet-rich ecclesiastical tradition and placing them above My name, above the "I Am the eternal law."*

*Under this backdrop of power of the "religious ruling guild," the state powers have been serving the idolatrous god into the present time.*

*At all times and into the present time, the idolatrous god was and is paid homage with adoration, a god who, at all times, promised and promises much to the believers—but until the present time, it was left at that.*

*Anyone who did not submit to the idolatrous god, the cult god, presenting it with offerings, was subjugated and sacrificed by the rulers of the respective system.*

*Entire hosts of like-attuned soldiers—like-attuned by the church and state power—fell upon children, women and men, raped children and women and slew whatever stood in their way, just as commanded by the respective requiem under an ecclesiastical flag.*

*The power of violence of the churches and state organs plundered and robbed entire peoples and, in a frenzy of blood, slew children, women and men in a bloody slaughter.*

*The idolatrous cult and its appendage, the corresponding state guild, had whole tribes bleed and starve to death through their mercenaries. They had children, women, the old and sick people tormented, tortured and raped—and this, in droves.*

*The Baal rulers held their so-called enemies in dark and moldy dungeons—regardless of whether they were women, children, the sick and weak, whether fathers and mothers, whether infants or young children.*

*Without consideration for the begging and pleading prisoners who were sick and emaciated from hunger, they flogged, tortured them at will and raped the gaunt women, girls and children by the thousands.*

*To get a piece of bread for the starving children, men and women turned into willing helpers and denouncers under the torturers' scepter—in the name of a punishing and chastising god: the idolatrous god of the Baal system of church and state power.*

*who I Am, will let rise the unatoned:*

*During the times of times, the heralds of God also fell victim to the idolatrous rulers and their idolatrous representatives, the religious declination—and thus, the violent criminals from the guild of priests and state power.*

*Nothing and no one was spared—unless those loyal to religion consorted with the sinister forces of power.*

*During the times of times and into the present time, the bloody sacrificial cults did not and do not pass over the animals, on the contrary. The animal world in factory farming is subject to a barbaric meat label for the lusts of the palate, that is, the conditioning of the palate. The brutality committed on countless animals took and takes on ever more forms.*

*The violation committed with the most brutal, cruel, raw violence against everything that lives— in the woods, fields and in the terrible animal barns—has become, and is, a generally condoned niveau, because the degenerated human being, the masses, sacrifice everything to their indifference.*

*This same indifference also prevails when it is about the institutions conducting animal experiments. Truly, the idolatrous god rages in these institutional establishments.*

*One atrocity follows the other.*
*Who encouraged such a thing?*
*Who is responsible for it?*

*The lack of conscience, the lack of feelings bear witness that the human being has long since become the accessory of the Moloch, who, since the times of times, has been pursuing his nefarious deeds in the cruelest of ways.*
*Yet what the person sows, he will reap.*

*With the cruel machinery of hell, which does not fail to have its brutal effect on fields and woods worldwide, the human being of cruelty turns the habitat sites of nature into sacrificial sites of the idolatrous god Baal.*

*Any and all poison that the human being gives to the animals in and on the Earth, including the animals in the waters, marks the planet Earth. The countless devices and equipment, as well, which are conceived with such contempt for life that hardly a living being can withstand them, are energies.*

*Any and all poison and the corresponding devices that are put to use for the extermination of the animal life and of the world of plants are energies, causes, which do not fail to have their effects.*

*The rifles in the woods and on the fields still have an appeal to the so-called hunters.*

*Where do these energies go, as well?*

*Where do all these horrible and death-bringing energies go?*

*To where do all these agonizing energies move and go, also according to the statements of your science that no energy is lost?*

*Where do the energies go—and what happens once the causality sets in?*

*esus of Nazareth brought to the people the God of the love for God and neighbor and the teaching of peace of His Sermon on the Mount.*

*Why does the cross with corpus have to serve the clan of priests and the state power for almost two thousand years, and the ritualistic use of church steeples in cities and villages?*

*These steeple-flags display what has been at all times and still is today, albeit, as a ritual scepter for all kinds of untruths under the term "Christian values."*

*In the patriarchal churches and on many a field stands the cross with corpus. Should that also be a sign of "Christian values"?*

*What are the so-called "Christian values"?*

*Are they the weapons that come from so-called "Christian countries" and thus, appropriate to kill and murder with?*

*Everything is based on energy. No energy is lost.*

*With this artificial trophy, the cross with corpus, the adversary from yesterday until today thinks that he has vanquished Me, the God of Abraham, Isaac and Jacob, the God of all the heralds of God, and that he has vanquished My Son, the Christ of God, whom I sent to you human beings and who, with His "It is finished," prevented the dissolution of the primordial substance and protected the core of being in every soul.*

*Although the trophy is erected in your churches and on many a field—it is as it is:*
*The Christ of God has accomplished Redemption for all ensouled human beings and souls. He is the Risen One and sits at My right hand. He comes in all splendor and glory, for the eternal Kingdom has prevailed.*

*After the long times of darkness, which humankind and the planet Earth still have before them, dawn will rise from the purified Earth. Then comes the time of the appearance of the Christ of God, who will establish His Kingdom with His own, which will very gradually cover the purified planet Earth: The Kingdom of Peace.*

*Now I, who I Am, announce the following concerning the last prophet: the prophetess in Me, who I Am, and who is in communication with My Cherub of Wisdom, once incarnated in Isaiah.*

*She, the present and last messenger of God, travelled to many countries to announce My message abroad, just as it took place many times in her home country. Here and there, hundreds of people came, if not to say thousands. They listened to the message of heaven and now hear it via radio and television.*

*How many heard and hear the message of heaven, and how many of them gave up their personal engagements, in order to found a people, a people in the Spirit of freedom and unity, in the love for God and neighbor?*

*Since My call to become a people of unity and freedom—with Abraham as well as with Moses, and now again, with the greatest prophetess since*

*Jesus of Nazareth—the majority of people all the way into the present time stayed true to their petty bourgeoisie and, as in Moses' time, loyal to the meat pots, for animal meat is directly and indirectly the source of energy for the idolatrous god Baal.*

*The synod of yesterday is the breach of today. The gates to the idolatrous god will not only close, but disintegration is the order of the day, for the Earth has become the enemy of humankind.*

*In all the times of times, the majority of people have antagonized and violated the planet Earth.*

*Now the Earth is rising against the evil race, against humankind, which, at all times since the Fall-system, from yesterday until today, shows its subservience to the idolatrous tyrants.*

*The demonic pedagogy is nothing new.*

*The Earth will yield what the religious guild with its appendage, the state authority, has entered into the Earth.*

*How does your science express it?*
*No energy is lost.*
*So is it—and so will it come!*

*Who recorded the energies of yesterday and the energies of today?*

*Since the Fall event, the energies are recorded in the so-called material cosmos, as well as on and in the Earth in a multi-layered way.*

*No energy is lost. For many souls, the energies are stored in various spheres of the finer-material cosmos. They are the inputs of energy, the personal aspects of erstwhile people, for what the former person sowed, the disembodied soul can now look at and remedy by clearing it up and atoning for it.*

*What cannot be remedied stays recorded in the Earth and comes back to the soul concerned, be it as a human being in the alternation of times of the respective incarnations, because no energy is lost.*

*What once was and is not yet atoned for stays present—yesterday and today.*

*The energies, the horrible deeds and works of humankind have not been atoned; thus, the people in all the times of times have made of the Earth their enemy. No energy is lost, not even those of the unatoned deeds of former times.*

*Since the Fall-system, the Fall-experts try to create a kingdom according to their standard and their goal, but into the present time it was only their will, but not their skill.*

*Thus, during the times of times, it stayed with their wanting.*

*Now, for the Fall-amateurs, it is found that it was too easy and too deceptive.*

*In all the times of times, many people were inclined to barbarity, because renouncing all ethics and morals—which let the lack of conscience become a means to an end—was and is self-assertiveness, and this, into the present time. The majority of people know about the Ten Commandments through Moses, but it was left at that up to the present time.*

# The Climate Change

*In the countries of this world much is discussed concerning the so-called climate change. Where does the climate change come from and who produced it?*

*To spark further discussions on how climate change is to be seen, all people need is a stone thrown into the water that draws many circles.*

*So that the all-too-human discussions do not get out of hand, I, who I Am, the All-Law of the Being, will clarify for the people where the climate change comes from.*

*Particularly these words "climate change" have many stanzas.*

*The many disharmonious stanzas come through the various discussions about the climate and the climate change and how this evil can be eliminated.*

*This is why the term "climate change" has become a melody, from which a song has been derived. And the song is the rendition of the catastrophic behavior of every single person, who contributed to bringing the planet Earth to the point of destruction in the shortness of time.*

*You people, keep listening to the song "climate change," which is your song, and if you want, trill along with the melody. Whatever you want, whether singing, trilling or merely listening—it is always you people, and no one else.*

*A short summary for better understanding:*
*By depleting and destroying the positive cycle of its energies at all levels, humankind has overridden the provider, the Earth.*
*Now, the Earth refuses to continue serving humankind, for humankind itself turned the Mother, the provider, the Earth, into an enemy.*
*The Earth with its countless resources energetically rises against humankind.*
*The Earth with its oceans, rivers, lakes and streams fights back. In many ways, the waters have become the deposit of carcass-like refuse. The so-called extinction of species—as the*

*human being calls it—shows the state of the plan-et Earth.*

*Death-bringing disaster goes over fields and through woods, over meadows and wetlands. The deserts and steppes are expanding everywhere. All that still breathes is subject to the system "destruction."*

*Everything else is only the remnants of life.*


*There is moaning and groaning on the Earth, above the Earth and in the murky waters. Under its energetic rape, the Earth groans the moan of death, and the death rattle in the waters is the melody in and on the Earth.*

*The melody and the song with its correspond-ing pitch are the disharmonious stanzas for each country—the climate change.*

*The agenda from the times to the times is thus called "climate change": the respective climate is the pitch differential. Humankind itself produced the melody and the respective catastrophic song for each country, and in the end, has also deliv-ered the corresponding score.*

*Thus, each country has contributed its stanza to the entire melody, "climate change." Each person sings and trills along. In this way, an orchestra emerged.*

*The conductors for each stanza of the respective country are the leaders in church and state. The inhabitants of the respective country trill along hoping that they will be spared, or that it would not hit them anymore, because their lifetime, their allotted years, would have expired.*

*Hardly anyone notices that they are singing or just trilling along because they are a part of it. Every soul, every person, measures and weighs themselves, and each one also determines things for themselves.*

*The scale weighs precisely. And hardly a person notices that they are a contemporary who yesterday, that is, in the times of times, was the same climate killer that they presently are.*

*The idolatrous parade of the idolatrous god understood how to wipe out the teaching of reincarnation, the teaching of the incarnation of souls in a human body. Otherwise, he would himself have been recognized as the lying Moloch of yesterday, who, at present, is only a floundering liar, trying to keep together his ever smaller flock of dependent idolatrous worshipers.*

*Despite the indifference of the majority of people from yesterday and today, it can no longer be stopped: Humankind turned the Earth, the oceans, all the waters into its enemy.*

*The word of science and the word of the idolatrous gods are valued by the believers.*

*Science says: "No energy is lost," and the idolatrous god opines: "God will set things right."*

*Both statements are correct, for I, who I Am, make all things new, also in terms of the energies, for no energy is lost.*

*However, it is important to bear in mind that in order to have everything become new, the old first has to pass away!*

*As stated, everything is based on energy!*

*Everything that in the times of times was inflicted and added onto the Earth, onto nature, the animals and plants, the waters and oceans, the atmosphere and the people, in terms of suffering and cruelties, crimes upon crimes, everything that was not amended, are unatoned energies in the Earth, on the Earth and above the Earth.*

*The time is ripe: I, who I Am make all things new.*

*I Am not the denouncer, merely the plaintiff, and I enumerate what during the times of times was not amended and not atoned for.*

*A dark and long cortege of denouncements is emerging, for the Planet Earth has been groaning since having to bear human beings.*

*The lamenting, moaning and groaning energies rise from the Earth and denounce humankind, and this, from country to country, from city to city, from place to place, from community to community, from village to village.*

*Everything that the souls in the worlds of the beyond, the purification planes, cannot bear, what befell them as human beings and what they did not cause themselves, are charges, which rise from the Earth as energies.*

*The countless fears of death of people before the blazing fires are energies. They rise as energies from the Earth and denounce.*
*The energetic denouncers are the countless victims, millions upon billions, whom the idolatrous cult of state and church have on their conscience. Energies upon energies rise from the Earth.*

*For better understanding, in terms of the perpetrators of yesterday and today:*
*The climate trills, the song, that draws from country to country, awakens the unatoned energies of the countless dead—the people who were once murdered, stabbed, impaled, tortured, hanged and shot, held in dungeons and, from country to country, beaten to death with the Cross of Peace before their eyes.*

*All the unatoned energies are rising—charges upon charges. People whose limbs were cut off in bestial ways, people who were mutilated and maltreated and left lying in prisons and dungeons, people who wasted away in pain and suffering as outcasts on the roads and pathways, people who were tortured to the point of death by agony rise as energies.*

*What does it look like in the present time?*

*The cortege of energetic accusers, which transfers the unatoned and stored energies of the murderous times of times to the perpetrators from long ago, gathers momentum.*

*Countless people who were burned at the stake, whole nations and tribes that were cruelly eradicated rise as energies and join the dark and ever longer cortege.*

*The fear of death of many children that were raped and brought to the Moloch and had to lose their lives as a burnt offering to the idolatrous god, rises as energies. Children who became "food victims" on the so-called Crusades rise as* energies and join the ever longer and grimmer cortege called "climate change."

The crimes of sexual offence against raped and violated women rise from the Earth as energies and join the cortege of horror.

All things unatoned rise from the repository Earth and point out the crimes of yesterday and today.

Everything, but absolutely everything—such as plundering, looting and thievery, slavery and serfdom, arson up to conflagrations, murder and genocide, war and manslaughter, including the murder of animals and the over-exploitation of nature—rises from the Earth.

Those who think they can decide about death, merely because they agree with the organ trade, decide about themselves and are present when the artificially declared dead rise as energies from the Earth.

All things unatoned, the causalities, causes upon causes, energies upon energies, rise and are directed against what is due to be atoned and *cleared up—in compensation, according to the law of sowing and reaping.*

*Energies upon energies rise from the Earth and join the dark cortege of horror.*

*he unatoned energies from the suffering of the many prophets and prophetesses, of the divine heralds, of the enlightened men and women, who at all times became victims of the cruelties, as well, carried out by the church and state power, join the ever-increasingly dark cortege.*

*All violent crimes rise as energy from the Earth and join the cortege of karmic energies.*

*Dark times will break in over the human race that rejected the word of the messengers from the Kingdom of God, for at all times, I, who I Am, taught the eternal law of love for God and neighbor.*

*Many people in all the countries of the Earth were kept in darkness, so that they would not see the light of eternity—for this reason, murderous death to the many bringers of light as well, to the messengers from the light.*

*The tactics of veiling and concealment are at all times also inherent in the power-holders of the state—the state power, the "beadle" of the powerful in the church.*

*The church clan is so powerful and power-obsessed, because the weak state takes advantage of the limitations of the people, who then offer up their fears to the church clan, which is insatiable. Much money is, of course, needed to hold a Requiem that has settled below, that is, which has its seat below, of which Jesus of Nazareth already spoke—it is the one who has need of the adoration, and today, all the more so: The father from below, who from the very onset of the Fall is a liar and a murderer. His abundance of facets dwindles, for the deception is being disclosed, not by Me, who I Am, the I Am, the Father-Mother-God, but by the former believers, who recognize the forces from below.*

*Irrespective of which arguments the church and state want to use to make excuses, it is as it is: Without atonement and making amends nothing can prosper, neither in the soul nor in the person nor in the deeds.*

*I Am the Eternal and the eternal law of love for God and neighbor that contains freedom.*

*Everything is weighed and allotted to each soul and each person according to its measure and weight.*

*The energies of the powerfully eloquent from the church, the state and their subordinates, also in terms of economy and society, from all those who participated and participate in the wars and famines, in the genocides and land-grabbing— these energies are all weighed and correspondingly justly apportioned by percentage. The corresponding seed is here and there, in the corresponding country, the harvest.*

*It seems as if there would be no end to the cortege of suffering, of murder, of the entirety of crimes of church and state, for when it comes to murder and violence, the cortege of the unatoned also draws through the oceans, rivers and lakes—nothing but violence, suffering, lingering illness and death. The energies of death of the marine animals and plants of every kind rise as corresponding energies and join the cortege of karmic energy.*

*No energy is lost, for the cortege of karmic energy that draws around the Earth grows ever longer, as do the dark times that have their melodies and their songs, called "climate change."*

*The climate in the course of times lets humankind gain an inkling of which stanza of the song will hit it today or tomorrow, regardless of which country, which place the present person of yesterday and of today has his part.*

*It is known—thus speaks the human being—that God's mills grind slowly, but justly. What the person sows—that is not atoned—he will reap.*

*Am, who I Am, who reveals much, but not all, not all the details from the inception of the Fall until the dawn, for the coming of My Son, of the Christ of God, once in Jesus of Nazareth, is announced.*

*The long and still grim cortege of suffering of the unatoned energies has not yet reached dawn, for the song of the climate change still has many stanzas, and each stanza points out and prompts atonement and making amends.*

*What should not be disregarded is that at all times humankind says: "Yesterday is yesterday, and today is today."*

*Verily, I Am, who I Am!*

*Your yesterday is the seed for your today—unless you have recognized your yesterday and have remedied your wrongdoings, your evil, with remorse and making amends. If not, then your yesterday is your today.*

*It is still as it is—hence, My word.*

*The black flag, which most people still hoist, is the dark drug of church and state power, which still presents itself with steeple dominance in many places only to lure the majority of people—and if there is no other way, then with the vow of baptismal water which means: bondage.*

*If the vow of faithfulness to the ecclesiastical powers slackens, then another one is pulled out of the preacher's pocket, which is: eternal damnation, eternal suffering in hell.*

*If such a vow were to be fact, that is, valid, then all those who demand such vows from their neighbor would be the first to find themselves in such an eternal suffering of hell, the church leaders and servants of power of ancient times, that is, the emperors, kings and state authorities of yesterday.*

*All of them would find themselves there again—not the many who became their victims, because they did not believe in the ecclesiastical phalanx, but rather opposed it.*

*If no energy is lost and everything is energy and the eternal law contains the possibility of* atonement and making amends—where, then, do these energies and the souls go?

Where are they? Do they sit on their tombs and wait for their resurrection on the Day of Judgment—or where are they?

Causality teaches this to them.

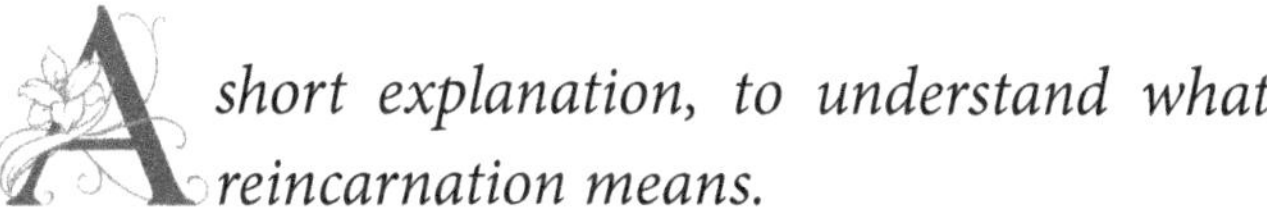A short explanation, to understand what reincarnation means.

Spoken through My instrument, My messenger, with three-dimensional words:

An eye for an eye, a tooth for a tooth.

What the person sows, the person will reap.

For the soul that bears the causes, this means: either reincarnation or expiation as a soul, perhaps in a long cycle, through which it has to bear the pain and the suffering, which, as a human being, it had caused to other people, or also with regard to the animals and nature.

*Where are the many people who can look at their seed in order to expiate the wrong committed, their horrible deeds?*

*Even if the disaster called religion rejects the reincarnation of the soul in a human body—for many souls, the incarnations become a gift of grace, if, as a soul, they look at their causal chain.*

*Millions upon millions of deceased people come as souls to re-embodiment, to incarnation, and are again born here and there, mostly in the countries, where the wrong of yesterday waits today for expiation—that is, where their causes from yesterday and today lie—in order to make amends there for what they caused long ago as human beings.*

*It simply is as it is:*

*Justice is the balance. If people yesterday had social prestige and were in the highest ranks, today, they come as simple citizens into the country in which their causes are presently active, in order to recognize what was still buried in their soul yesterday, that is, in previous existences—thus, the causes—or, according to their dimension and weight, to bear their effects.*

*Therefore, what was yesterday can be the today.*

*The karmic cortege, which will continue to move around the Earth until much has been atoned for, brings many things to light, including the unspeakable suffering of the animals, also in terms of animal cannibalism, which, in many cases, still has not come into effect. The karmic cortege, the corresponding energies bring everything to light.*

*Reincarnation is thereby a gift of grace; it is the mercy, for the expiation on the pathways of the soul can truly be painful soul journeys.*

*The dark and long cortege still has its chapters.*

*Among others, one chapter is significant:*

*Atonement or making amends in good time, whereby the earthly word "in good time" is important, because the cortege of working things off has again gathered speed.*

*The melodies of the climate change, the stanzas that move from one country to another, are becoming ever clearer and weightier in content, and thus, also the effects, the causalities from yesterday and today, which, in the end, each person is himself.*

*From country to country, the quality of the causes will show different effects, for the soul of a person who passes away today can be born, that is, incarnate, in another country tomorrow, depending on the quality of yesterday.*

*e it as it may:*

*The path—whether as soul or human being—gives the direction: either upward or to an incarnation. The grim works of yesterday that are cleared up, that is, remedied, today show the way to the light, which is eternity.*

*Unfortunately, for still a long time on this Earth, the cortege of death, that is, of murder, will show what needs to be atoned.*

*However, depending on the corresponding country, the chapter of long darkness on this Earth will gradually brighten, and it will get sunnier, because the Earth will also become more light-filled.*

*An Earth that becomes more light-filled signifies the spiritual dawn and the beginning of the New Era.*

*A virgin Earth will emerge under the sign of My Son, the Co-Regent of the Kingdom of God, who, as Jesus of Nazareth, announced His coming: "I come soon."*

*Then, the sinful temples and steeples with their idolatrous god are shattered. All the black flags of the Baal priesthood are destroyed. No religious flag waves anymore.*

*People of the New Era find the true God in their peace-loving nature and, on the new Earth, build the Kingdom of Peace under the Sign of the Lily—Sophia—the purity and freedom of the love for God and neighbor.*

*A word to the supporting pair of divine Wisdom, the third basic power before My throne:*

*My daughter, whom I entrusted to the Cherub of eternal Wisdom—truly, again and again, and still again!—briefly revealed, those were your incarnations, in which the Prince of Wisdom, the Regent, also called the Cherub, accompanied you.*

*He stayed at your side—He is at your side—the duality of Wisdom before the throne of the seven primordial powers, of the Father-Mother-Being.*

*The supporting pair of the eternal Wisdom carried and carries the banner of peace: The Cherub, once in Isaiah on the Earth, and his dual with various names according to the ages, now the prophetess and emissary of God, Gabriele.*

*The banner is erected and stands for the Christ of God, who, as Jesus of Nazareth, announced His coming in the Spirit of His eternal Father, who I Am.*

*In the times of times, before Abraham and after Abraham, there were always faithful people gathered around the woman who carried the divine law and taught it.*

*As at all times, the representatives of the black flag were among the people, in order to destroy everything that even just gave the impression of serving the Free Spirit, God, who I Am.*

*The incarnated Wisdom sustained the lily of purity, the law of the love for God and neighbor, from incarnation to incarnation and taught what was possible, although she had much to suffer under the ballistic regime.*
*She sustained and sustained; at her side was the Prince of Wisdom, the Cherub. Again, they sustained together and sustained it into the*

*present time. The gateway of the Lily, the Wisdom, under the sign of Sophia is opening.*

*In many facets, she taught the life for the New Era in the Kingdom of Peace in coming. The Cherub, the Prince, that is, the Regent of Wisdom, revealed in many schooling hours, how the Land of Peace could take on shape and form, the light intensity, which announces the coming of the Christ of God: "I come soon."*

*From the Spirit, the Work of the Deed of Wisdom in Me, the eternal Wisdom continues to work, even then, when the fiend still permeates the polluted atmosphere. Via the prism suns, the light of the Christ of God is already shining.*

*In the Spirit of eternity, the exalted woman will appear, of whom it is written, and who erects, in unity with her spirit dual, the throne of the appearance, the sign of the Co-Regent of the Kingdom of God, who, at the side of the eternal Father-Mother-Being as Co-Regent, reflects His light of revelation for the New Era, which shows the transition into the Kingdom of God.*

*In the divine Being and conscious of their responsibility, the supporting pair of the divine Wisdom is active, the third basic power before the throne of the Eternal, who I Am.*

*During the decades, the exalted woman, the Lily, Sophia, taught the people what the Christ of God calls to them yesterday and today:*
*"Come all to Me, the Christ of God, I want to lead you!"*

*The dragon is defeated. He has fallen to the Earth and will be transformed by the Earth that is cleansing itself.*

*The Earth is cleansed for the most part of the mold and smell of corpses, of depravity and idolatry. The Earth receives a divine garment.*

*The Eternal, who I Am in unity with My Son, the Co-Regent of the Kingdom of God and the Regency of the eternal Wisdom, calls into this world:*

*Indeed, it is done. A new heaven and a new Earth emerge through the "Let there be."*
*I, who I Am, make all things new.*

*Already now, the call of the Christ of God goes around the Earth, and all people who bear the cross on their brow, the sign of peace and of love, hear the call of the Christ of God, which says: "Where two or three are gathered in My name, there am I, in the midst of them."*

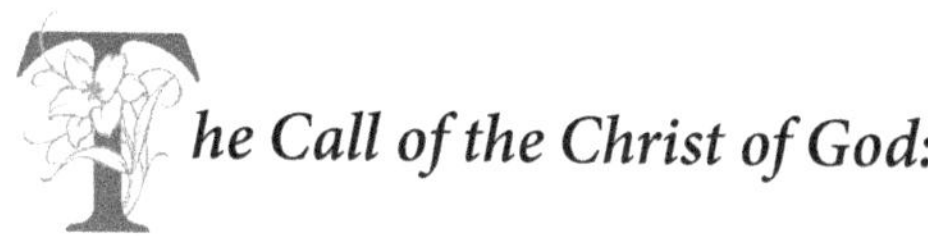

*he Call of the Christ of God:*

*"The signs are visible, the appearance*
*leads the way, the dawn*
*reveals to My own the light-filled day*
*and the New Era.*

*I Am in God, My Father,*
*the eternal Being, His Son.*
*The Regency pair of the eternal Wisdom,*
*makes manifest My coming.*

*In this awareness of the New Era*
*for peace-loving people:*

*The Christ of God, who I Am in the eternal*
*Father-Mother-Being,*
*in God, who is the eternity!"*

We will be glad to send you our free catalog
with free excerpts on many different topics:

**Gabriele Publishing House—The Word**

North America: P.O. Box 2221, Deering, NH 03244
Toll-Free No.: 1-844-576-0937

**www.Gabriele-Publishing-House.com**

Germany: Max-Braun-Str. 02, 97828 Marktheidenfeld
International Orders: +49 (0) 9391-504-843

**www.Gabriele-Publishing.com**